WE ALL HAVE A HERITAGE

Part II of "The People" Series

Story by Sandy Lynne Holman
Illustrated by Lela Kometiani

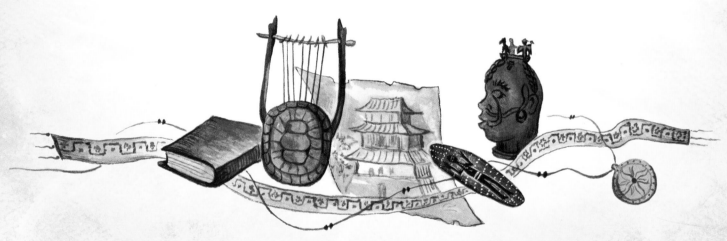

To all the beautiful children of the world
Always know that you are special.

Especially for our children
Latisha, Jasmine, Veronica, Monique, Monaé, Anna and Alexander.

By Sandy Lynne Holman, award winning author of
Grandpa, Is Everything Black Bad?
Published by The Culture C.O.-O.P.

10 9 8 7 6 5 4 3 2 1
Publisher's Cataloging In Publication Data
Holman, Sandy Lynne.
We all have a heritage / story by Sandy Lynne Holman ; Illustrated by Lela Kometiani
Davis, CA : Culture C.O.-O.P., 2002. SAN 299-3260
p. cm.
Summary: An illustrated story of children from diverse backgrounds who learn and celebrate the fact that we all have a Heritage and that we have a lot in common.
ISBN 0-9644655-2-3
1. Ethnicity - Juvenile poetry. 2. Self-perception - Juvenile poetry. 3. Blacks - fiction I. Title II. Kometiani, Lela.
PZ7.H663 W4 2002 2001-094307 CIP

Grandpa, Is Everything Black Bad?

By Sandy Lynne Holman
Illustrated by Lela Kometiani

In part I of our "The People" Series, *Grandpa, Is Everything Black Bad?*, Montsho questions the goodness of his black skin because he sees so many black things in his life that are bad; bad guys on TV wear black, black cats bring bad luck, and people wear black to funerals. Montsho learns of his proud heritage from his Grandfather, whose wise words and magical drum help Montsho to identify himself with his African roots. *Grandpa, Is Everything Black Bad?* ends with Montsho asking his Grandfather whether white people have a heritage too. His Grandfather replies, "All people do." Thus, Montsho's lesson continues as he learns that *We All Have A Heritage*. Join Montsho as his Grandfather introduces him to the world.

We all have a Heritage,
yes this is true.

It doesn't matter if your skin is black, white,
yellow, brown, red, purple or blue.

All of us have a history
where people did great things

And most of us came from Countries
where there were once Kings and Queens.

We all have ancestors
who lived a long time ago

Some we may remember
and some we don't know.

We all have special traditions
and a place from whence we came

And people from the past
gave most of us our last names.

We all have a Heritage, yes this is true.
It doesn't matter if your skin is black, white,
yellow, brown, red, purple or blue.

We all have special languages
so that we can all speak

And everyone celebrates holidays
that make certain days unique.

We all eat delicious foods
prepared in various ways

And all cultures have music
to help us dance through the days.

We all have traditional clothes
that honor our rich roots

And many cultures have musical instruments
like drums, guitars or flutes.

We all have a Heritage, yes this is true.
It doesn't matter if your skin is black, white,
yellow, brown, red, purple or blue.

Did you know that if you travel
there is so much you can explore?

You can see people using their talents
to make things you've never seen before.

Whether we travel to the North,
to the South, the East or the West

We can all explore our Heritage
and see the world at its best.

You might learn certain customs
to tell you how things are done

Or you could see different activities
that are done just for fun.

We all have a Heritage, yes this is true.
It doesn't matter if your skin is black,
white, yellow, brown, red, purple or blue.

Do you know what else is amazing
about you and me too?

If you look at our insides,
we are the same through and through.

Even though we may be different colors
with different looks on our faces,

We are all still just human beings
who happen to come from different places.

We can learn about each other
and the different things that we do

And we can share what we have in common,
both in me and in you.

Because we all have a Heritage, yes this is true.
It doesn't matter if your skin is black, white
yellow, brown, red, purple or blue.

By sharing our Heritage with each other
we can learn from the start

How to respect different people
and keep love in our hearts.

Look for the previous title in this series by this author...

Grandpa, Is Everything Black Bad?

Look for the next title by this author...

Grandma Says Our Hair Has Flair

Would you like the author to visit your school?

Interested in customized diversity training services by the author?

See inside back cover for these and other details.

If you enjoyed this book, consider buying one for a child as a donation or a gift.

If you are interested in obtaining additional copies of this book or are interested in other products and services offered by The Culture C.O.-O.P., please contact us in one of the following ways.

Toll-free orders only: 1-877-COLORS-7
Business inquiries: (530) 792-1334
Email: info@CultureCo-Op.com
FAX: (530)-753-8511
Web: www.CultureCo-Op.com
US Mail: P.O. Box 463, Davis, CA 95616

Sample services offered by The Culture C.O.-O.P.

- Motivational/Keynote Speaking
- Diversity Trainings
- Character Education Trainings
- Author Visits
- Book Signings
- Teambuilding Workshops
- Communication Skills Seminars
- Change Management Seminars
- Positive Youth/Adult Development
- Staff Retreats
- Mentor Program Development
- Alcohol/Drug Prevention Program Development

Please call us with your questions, comments and requests for services.